Elegies

Lucy,

Herewith Elegies

You get a mention!

love

Cedric

Elegies

Cedric Cullingford

Published by www.lulu.com

© Copyright Cedric Cullingford 2018

ELEGIES

All rights reserved.

The right of Cedric Cullingford to be identified as the author of this work has been asserted in accordance with the Copyright, Designs and Patents Act 1988.

No part of this publication may be reproduced, stored in a retrieval system, or transmitted, in any form or by any means, electronic, mechanical, photocopying, recording or otherwise, nor translated into a machine language, without the written permission of the publisher.

This is a work of fiction. Names and characters are a product of the author's imaginations and any resemblance to actual persons, living or dead, events and organisations is purely coincidental.

Condition of sale

This book is sold subject to the condition that it shall not, by way of trade or otherwise, be lent, re-sold, hired out or otherwise circulated in any form of binding or cover other than that in which it is published and without a similar condition including this condition being imposed on the subsequent purchaser.

ISBN 978-0-244-44299-6

Book formatted by www.bookformatting.co.uk.

Contents

Part 1 Elegies 1

Daybreak 2

The turning of the night 5

The dawning 7

Highly commutable 9

Earthtime 11

Wrong wiring 13

Churchyard 15

Monuments 17

As it is on earth 19

Heat 21

The neighbour's children 23

Airmen 25

The philosophy of want 27

The power of nature 29

Colour 30

Olives 32

The edges of sea 34

Early evening 36

The lineaments of stone 38

The lost symbol 40

The breath of autumn 42

Cars passing 44

The song of the night 46

Like leaves 48

Driving past signals 49

The slumber of silence 51

Night chambers 53

Street lights 55

The sounds of achievement 57

Part 2 Lamentations 59

Foreign Legions 60

Fishers of men 62

Bodies 64

Goose steps 66

The burning of the dead 68

The moon in daylight 70

Mourning's monument 72

Paradise on earth 74

Homeland 76

Displacement 78

Interior decorations 80

Longing 82

The other world 84

Casino 86

Under the sea 88

Part 1 Elegies

Daybreak

Slowly the town settles and the last revellers
expand on their excitement in the night
     their plaintive joy
joins the first cries of the seagulls
as they dream of vast futures
     and forget their past

the sleeping are still fading in their silent lives
like leaves folded in their own shade

in the circles of the street light the rain
reflects the spreading ripples of the dawn
     on the still puddle
before a car destroys it

we can almost see
     a dawning before the dawn arrives
that moment we all know
     and cannot place
for it cannot be measured like time

that moment when the light is artificial
     and the rain
drops individually
maintain in their rounded sides
the street light and the night
that single window and the curtain drawn

that moment when
before the end of night has been so much as
    hinted at
before the electric light that seeps out of the room
    fades
losing its power to create
    its own small world
shining on the smooth sides of each rain drop
    sliding down the glass

that moment which is colour more than light
when the shouts that spill over the windows
    of the last parties
have discovered a new tone
    and the songs
that sustained another pool of late night drunks
asserting that the night would never end
    that they would better it

are now reflecting on the cries that come
    when pleasure turns to melancholy
and like an ambiguity of seagulls
join their cry
    deprived
        deprived

but before the night
is almost over and the last hug
    is received and the traffic
noises its way along the seafront
    faster in its darkness
than the day would allow

there is that moment when the world
has turned on itself and all the
horror of the heart is made as clear
      as wrestling with angels
and the world outside is for a moment here.

The turning of the night

In the darkness comes the stirring
    the whimper of lost souls
    the crying of the young exposed
on the hillsides of their parents' minds

these terrors have no inner meaning but are cries
that are incessant
    unambiguous
        and cruel
that join the brisk anticipated call
of the passing seagull
    in its ridicule

like decay that hibernates inside us
disease sleeping in the hollow of the eye
to terrorise identity
and make it strange
    unkind
        and unfamiliar
incessant wth renewal

the night anticipates the terrors of the day
and asks humiliating questions
    for which there is no time to prepare
and even when I try to answer
    no one will hear

the perennial tests of childhood
    climb into the inner ear
in rows of individual dread
as if blind punishment anticipated crime

but dawn is when the terrors
are supposed to go to sleep
    or at least be silent
        if not silent then ignored
or drunk to oblivion

the people of the dreams are anonymous
    they have their jobs to do
taking particles of hope that float
in the vast and unforgiving whole
    like a thief

they are the perpetual interference with the soul

knowledge is no protection
but it creates an ache for comfort and relief.

The dawning

When the night at last is sucked away
    like a tide turning
    and the black water
outlined by the foam
    the moon illuminates
blends into itself

    there is a hint of sun
or not so much of sun exactly
    but sun mitigated
not so much sun as light
    not so much light as that
presence which the light intends
when without self-consciousness
    each of us is still

the sound of waves hoeing shingle is replaced
    by the more sustained
shingling of a lorry steaming through the rain
and turning over ripples in the road
    and that slowly
fading pool of light the headlamps make
becomes part of a larger life

no longer isolated
like a driver in his cab
    anonymous in his own light
but creating a need
to talk as well as listen

when all the sounds
the sea and rain make similar
the water revolving on the shore
    the turning of the wheels
there is no turning back the waters
    of the dark

but there is that moment when
the light that has been centred in the room
    is diffused
and turning ripples on the road are
more like shore for all their struggling

then in that most bleak
of long time hours that makes
    each person realise
they do not know what kind of day is breaking
we understand
    a little more
of what is dream and what is real

it is that moment when
the night is at its zenith
before changing with the dawn

    a new beginning
a new day daring to be born.

Highly commutable

The hours that anticipate awakening
from the turbulence of dreams
    fall between
obscurity in individual sleep
and the rancour of collective lives
between the unimaginable distance
    that is heaven
and the undercurrents of imperfect earth

the human traffic of the day slips
between the signals that direct
    and those that blame
individuals in their quiet desperation
where the awakening world
bubbles up as if through water
    like quarrels surfacing
finding themsleves between
conflicting signals
    and the bright lights of
hindsight suddenly cancelled

those driven by their lonely wakefulness
dream of others in their loneliness
    those they listen to
        and those they hear
those with whom they thought
    or promised
they were near

some can survive unkindness
    the misleading signals
intensions misunderstood deliberately
the undercurrents of obscure discontent

others rumble through the night and day
    in congestions of advice
holding on to journeys as long as they will last
    fearing their arrival
dreading the reverberations of the past.

Earthtime

When the darkness is no longer visible
and the earth emerges from its own background
    like a spell

we cannot know the moment
when the trees become their outlines
    and the shadows retain the same shape
where they fell

the moment of undawning
the light sweat of leaves
the bright berries that were once
    at one with flowers
still await our reluctant noticing
    like a threat

bulbs emerge from the forgotten
weight of water
and the missing stars evoke
the hidden corners of childhood

to undermine the longings
    that haunt cut grass
the dread of what is coming
the ambiguities of the new day
that seeks to diminish me
    with its own alien integrity

until the unsafe obscurity of darkness
and the absence of what is fair
    disappears like dew
and the bleak emptiness of night
has also vanished
    like despair.

Wrong wiring

I am the human discovered in a field
leaning on yielding sheaves of wheat
    a wood for background
as in a picture
    familiar as elms

the picture is of quiet countryside
    ladders leaning into apple trees
with fields to succour them
    in the safe shadows
that forgotten trees once cast
    comforted by the distant past

I am displaced
    by new machineries of thought
intruding messages of unknown miseries
    far from my own
by the corrugated edges of the field
    the trees that lie
crumbling slowly like asbestos
    the concrete that dents the plough

lost in the panoply of broken boughs
vast technologies replacing thought
    and now
the manic actions
of combined harvesters
    that are never human
        and never tired

they tell me I am wrongly wired

I miss the familiar mechanics of the everyday
    like wind and rain
the news that remains at bay
    far enough away to be dealt with

I long for the comfort of the turning page
    predictable as age
leaning on bookshelves
or the trees from which they came

but am like an old moon
    misted with the last of the rain
like an engraving
outlined with the black and white of night

there are the new moulds of thought
    new templates of reflection
but although I know that I am tied
to the eternal past
    and it is never time to go

can humanity be out of tune
or was it always so?

Churchyard

In the shadows that make up a churchyard
tombs await the interference of the roots
of yews that will one day
      undermine them

and the weatherworn lettering
      of long forgotten names
pass into the anonymity of fading stone

the weight of years will seep through
      the privacy of bones
will undercut the ordinary
ageing of the everyday
      and mark the end of innocence

these modest monuments to love
      if not to love at least to
sullen recognition
      or to fading memory

these are also individual souls
      waiting
to be undone by ivy
forever mixed with the anointing sun

they follow the earthly lines of fate
as seagulls follow the plough
      as if to be uplifted

here are the ordinary and the everyday
the loved and the forgotten
those who never made a mark
but in their death
    have left their shadows
in the unrefining letters of their name
    moulding on lichened stone

singled out
like shadows on the wall
    one by one

shadows defined by the uplifting sun.

Monuments

Church monuments endow the dead
with power in their almost perfect
shrouds of virtue
    their unprecedented grace

their titles and accomplishments
embrace the casual eye
    as if the great and powerful
remained in place

to think such people lived!

the empty thrones of windows
draw in the sun
and stain the monumentss with virtues not their own

and on their tombs
as if awaiting some uplifting
small carved birds attempt
    to fly
    one by one
above each successive gaze

perhaps their stone embodiments
unlike the realities of love and shame
are the nearest they could ever get to fame

and we are left with their aspirations
thinking about what will never be achieved
    or if achieved
        then still forgotten

diurnal sunlight still seeps in
like spasmodic visitors
    who cast their eyes
on the artifice of stone

and notice no particular virtue
    no particular crime
but temporary power
and the fashion of the time.

As it is on earth

The blue sky is crossed by the white smoke
of a disappearing aircraft
    like a vandal's scratch marks

it beckons like an unknown heaven

the blank space is bland as freedom
but the emptiness is unreality
hiding darkness crossing the light of time

appearances shield us from the outer reaches of the earth
    like the egotistical sublime
we seek the freedom of the skies
    and its unsublime reality

hope like an empty window
beckons us to escape the darkness
but we are constrained by earth

the weight of the universe
holds down the compost that our lives become

the flattened soil that
fuels the vegetables
    with anonymous intent
nurtured by its own obscurity

makes us seem like old vines
branches propped by crutches
    rusting nails
decaying fruit weighed down
by nets of heavy air
struggling with purgatorial pain

the earth decays beneath our feet
the angels are in the darkness of the deep
    without form

so we go to earth
struggle to survive false witnesses
    like a never ending birth
and wait for the coming storm.

Heat

The hours stretch like a half awakening dog
as if there were no such
    particulars as time

the stray dogs find their cover in
    imagined shadows and lie down
in the desultory sleep
    of latent discontent

even the shadows vibrate with heat
    and lethargy accumulates
like minute particulars of decay

the neighbours open another tin of meat
    while the swarming radio
fills the fetid room with sound
until its hum accumulates around their feet

the used plates are accomodated in the sink
and empty tins reveal
    their jagged edges
like an open mouth
    of once carniverous teeth

the wasted day is emptied of its possibilities
there is nothing left for them to do
    no will

no thought of what each passing minute means
whilst the trees decay
and stillness empties time
    of every good intention

the neighbour's fridge is almost empty
the unread papers piled against the door
    unwanted journals
laying bare their information
    like a swarm of flies
where the ephemera of the latest news
    like lies
have blended into the diaspora of air.

The neighbour's children

The neighbour's children are lounging in the street
waiting for something to affect them
    like an idea
flies are making feasts out of the heavy air

the children will never leave

there is no weather here beneath the sky
the windows are a spiders dream
the neighbour's children do not listen
    even to themselves
not even plotting the pleasures of decay
they do not even think of food
    or something to destroy
having nothing left to say

the children spread themselves
    unwanted
attack the surface of the road
    and hum their tunes
accumulate more stones
to make them into weapons
for which they have no particular use

I wonder if this is their perfect moment
they will one day long for
    without a sense of threat
without the sense of an ending
    and its accumulating dread
in the spurious peace that waits
for what must one day happen
    only when they are not ready

the neighbour's children will blend
    like dust
into the heat
waiting for the end.

Airmen

A thin white line in the sky
    that fades
is all that is left of a plane
    passing into some better place than this
as if it were lifted into bliss

in the very centre of ourselves
the inner haunts of childhood
we think of souls who fly
who do not stumble on their own
    impediments
they appear far more secure
    heading for another world
of twinkling lights and time

the souls who fly there
are the air's propensity for renewal
they soak up the weight of dust
to dust as subtly as belief
in the constant generation of the air
    so high
        so immaculate
            and clean
                into the tempting distances
into spaces that
free them from confinement

    they are in the air without contamination
        going to a better place

    they have seen the security of night
        its mercival release
from the awareness of another world
        the twinkling lights of time

like the comfort of the stars
their quiet sounds absorb
        the nights of troubles
            they have had on earth

they make their distance seem
the very centre of the home
        at least my own
in the inner haunts of childhood
in a life of pure mind
        without contaminants
            without fear

all I know of the world beyond
        their world
is the wonder of it
        as they disappear.

The philosophy of want

The days of understanding are past

in the deep waters of society
the claws of individuals
clutch at each others throats
    in trying to prove
that they are right
and have the might to prove it
    until they drown

deep down
in the pit of oceans
where the soundless bubbles
creep up to the noisy surfaces
rising like a slow awakening
    into the troubles of the night

the fish appear
lost in shoals like
crowds controlled in the shimmer of
dancers in a line
    in moving unity
    in sharing dreams
        like individual souls
part of the layers of a better world
    anonymous as number

each particle of fish might not seem aytonymous
but each is in its own horizon in the world
    not ground to earth
not limited to the seam of
    flat reality
the simple arithmetic of limited dimensions

but each can rise and rise
and slide through all perspectives
    with the ease of flying
with the freedom of those souls
who have no thought of dying

each fish is an awakening
from the imaginary role of individual hate
joined together in their
    unselfconscious silences
        their shoals of territory
and their fate

they have their inner peacefulness
    whilst all around the sea
surges and displays
the triumph of the greater whole
silently and free
a reminder of lost harmony
    of thinking individul souls.

The power of nature

Spring's insistent greenery
    as the forest
bursts from underground
to spill its hidden roots
over the many shades and seemings

is not easy to admire
like the struggle with the forest
    of our own minds

wishing we could see
through the mass of thorns and leaves
that impenetrable focus of obscurity
    the micro climate of the eye
the self-centre of grief

brute force is no substitute for the unbidden
    complexity of grace
that curdles with its own
    peculiar green purpose to be free

climbing up the darkness of the tree
    blending individual rights
        like selfishness
into a shared whole
    the stamina of earth
rising upwards
the osmosis of the soul.

Colour

The afternoon merges into soil
and colours shift according to slight
    nudges of time
that take each pigment of light
    into the evening
as subtly as trying to keep still

the flowers accommodate themselves to blue
absorbed by individual petals into
new and unexpected forms
    of incompatability
        until
the colours cannot quite be trusted

    for us
there is no natural process of decay
but a series of moments
beyond a simple ending
    beyond the promise of another day

it does not lie in us to trust
    in distant stars
but accept what we see
    as earth accepts the trees

for us
the passing beauty
of the change of light
    becomes a type of permanence
through the natural shift
    of darkness and decay

for us it is the sight connects
    not roots
not only flowers
that make their colour
display what is for ever inward

for us there is belief
that there will always be
new flowers
    changing as they must
imperfect but fully there

like trust.

Olives

Olives celebrate survival
as if old age were an achievement
    in the toil of day to day
seeking nourishment
from the strange soil of the unknown below

when sunlight gossamers the groves
    and filters them with nets
that spider their way between the branches
the stillness absorbs
    every particle of day

the movement of light along each web
    is a moment
when the sun has had its say
illuminated
like an unexpected stay
    of judgement

when the olives lend their taste to wine
    absorbed in sun and soil
to make us feel more powerful
    more overflowing
with unspent time

olives make those moments when
all can be savoured
    unlike a lifetime

where relishing the breeze
    the wine
        and the turquoise sea
becomes at last
    one moment

filtered out of leaves
    in a beauty of completeness
without question
    without strife
        and without haste

is everything else in life a waste?

The edges of sea

The light is fading
and the sea at last contained
    in its own emptiness
its surfaces
spread across all distances
    like corruption

only the powerful survive
against the sea's
    slow
inevitable sense of void defining itself
    like an afterthought
reacting to the slip
stream of the first pure drops of seeming
    more permanent
        more secure

lurching on the surface of the real
where the world is undermined
    by water
which like power
    is oblivious to catastrophe

beneath the cold transplanted waves of the sea
lie the lost landscapes of memory
    where a shelf of rock awaits
the careful joining of the land
    and me

always on the edge of drowning.

Early evening

When the sun sets and the landscape settles
    and the leaves like closed curtains
try to keep the darkness out
and blackbirds have finished their last rounds
    putting anguish in its place
the grasses nudge into the same colour
    to make an imperfect harmony of grace

then there is that moment
    when all seems one
under the great encircling sky
    discomfort is undone
and in that perfume of pure air
    like anticipated wine
the moment spreads like privilege

as if there were a recognition
    of a hallowed world
that fosters all inclusion
    and even this
particular soul is part of it

that moment is
    like the tickle of the wine
that spreads
    with a benign decay
as often as impossible
like the moment of the sun
in its subtle sinking
into the twilight where the blackbirds sang

there is then that pang
    of happiness

we long for the perfect moment
the landscape that connects the soul
    to a simpler universe
connects the body with what is beyond
    the anguish of the everyday

when the encircling sun
and the wine's embrace
    creates what seems forgetfulness
but is a perfect harmony of grace.

The lineaments of stone

A church can seem as innocent
    as an old film
where lack of colour indicates
    unblemished attitudes
blessed with close proximity to ignorance

    a tomb of ancient stone
where monuments express
    in marble mourning
all we need to know
    of angelic or of human excellence
for the admiration of the crowd below
the winged angels look down
    on their admirers
on battered flags that hang
like medals of the wars
    long lost
on fading flowers of commemoration
where the colours of display
    fade in a familiar grey
of a half remembered world

the watchers cannot know
    the true significance
of the array of tombs
anointed by decay
    in which there is no anguish

where like an old film that can be run
      backwards
the arrows of medieval war
extract themselves from the now unwounded
      and fly like seagulls
back into the snug enclosure of the bow
into the past

the only certainty we know.

The lost symbol

Fire and wind
are natural followers of bombs
    that make a rubble of the past
and hunt down humans for impermanence

so many burdens on the earth
such weight upon the eyes
    one would not think it possible
that any sign of what was human
    could arise
from such destruction
from the last remnants of humanity
    the broken compost of time

and yet
    on every pile of rubble
the earth turned upside down
    the double digging of the bombs

against the odds
    against the suspension of terror
one sign of lost humanity
makes its way upwards

through the tatters of respectability
     singly
through the layers of pain
through the wallpapers of the past
the interior chambers of the everyday
     that kept the darkness out

the enamel pot
that trivial symbol of necessity
     the final image of the broken home

has its presence there
     above the rubble
some small spot of triumph
     of the ordinary
like the touch of the lost past
coming to the surface of a dream

the potholes in every ache of road
     that expanded to embrace
whole houses in their fold
where only the blind eye of night
     can comprehend
what bombers left behind
recycling not just earth like compost
but their hold on people's lives

as if all humans are expendable

when there is such constant change
will there be nothing of the last remains
     of lost humanity
but some absurd symbol of oblivion?

The breath of autumn

As the stars appear
    reluctantly
and the cold is sucked into the soil
the night air seeps into souls
    like a virus

with the ebbing of the day we hear
the spirits of decay
    and sense not see
the owl of night patrolling hedges

and in the first grey ignorance of the evening
there is a sign
    a hint of colour running away
    from spent reminders of the day
dreams we wanted to delay
    not dreams but pressing images
        not images but fate
the shiver not of body but of mind
the dread that follows the policeman's knock
    before bad news

for that moment in the day
    when all colours are at one
the weight of each autumnal leaf
    like flags fading into tatters
on the branches of church walls
die in competition for the sun
spent leaves like waves that can no longer wait
    to break upon the shore
fall from view

we watch them go
as the wind and cold
    regain their own particular territory
and take the place of leaves that have been
bullied until they lost their hold.

Cars passing

In the quiet of the night outside
    beyond the bedroom curtain
a car drives through the darkness
and its light rushes the opposite way
    fast across the ceiling

those passing by
seem safe in their enclosures

busying to some other place
where they will enter
the welcome strangeness of others
    the centre of their inattention

all we know of the world beyond
    is the wonder of it

here the curtains take on different shapes
    of light and shadows
in a show of disappearances

and we think of precious times
between the quarrels
    and the painful letters
the angry gesture that is
    hidden so it is not seen
the jealous mantras of what might have been

here the curtains take on different shapes
       of light and shadows
in a show of disappearances

the night has gaps for dreams
that make the curtains move
with an imagined light
       taking with it
like the lightest kiss
all the illuminations that the night conceals
those imagined unconfinements of adventure
       and of unimaginable bliss.

The song of the night

Out of the silent dead of night
a single voice is crying
    like an absconding angel
pleading for attention
an outcast in the uniform of failure
    and a prisoner of dread

singing the song that the defeated sing
    out of sight
without conviction

with no one listening but other fugitive angels
    who have better things to do
than succour failures in their
constant and uncivil wars

it is a song that penetrates the
questionable comfort of the dark
    snug as a pillbox

while searchlights cross the skies
and the rumble of more important business
    continues in its own time
like distant thunder
or the routines of crime

the song of the night is a soldier
creeping home after a defeat
     shabby as a battledress
the tatters of sadness
singing for lost hope
     out of the obliterated past
trying to overcome the dread
     of being forgotten
without the excuse of being dead.

Like leaves

The leaves attended to the sun
until their clinging dependency on trees
was over and their day was done
      they became the sacrament of soil

and when the leaves
      simply fell away
          and joined
accumulating layers of decay
like an early autumn
      contaminating thought
they become no longer single but a crowd
a host of all the fallen that will arise
      like old souls to be
the vast whole of anonymity

so when certainty cannot be found
      like a mislaid wallet
there is nothing to be mourned
about our own autumnal falling
      the letting go
not accepting expendability
that is our own

all is as one when
winter turns up like a policeman
      and at last the tragedy is done.

Driving past signals

Drivers in their private spaces
    in the darkness of the night
manipulate the wheels that they control
enclosed within their own illuminations
    of the outer world
turning left or right
to pass by other private worlds
    that sleep at night

the drivers pass on signals
forestalling arguments with good intentions
as if all signals that they make
    steer between
others in their sheltered anonymity
and the assertions of their individual place

it is not always so
some can take their own unkindness with them
their anger ever watchful
    for the chance to take offence
resentment burning like a traffic accident

the lights are flashing and the drivers go
from the lit streets into the darkness
where they follow their own lights
    and they know
        letting passions fade
that only their own signs guide them
    making a brief impression
where the dark road leads them
like good intentions
    out of sight

we are all long distance drivers
signalling vainly in the night

The slumber of silence

The town reverberates to the machines that hum
mimicking the constant murmur of electricty
    like quiet sounds of fear
the artificial music of the sun
blending humans
    who invented noise
into one

as if there could be no more silences

the individual noises sway
    like background music
masking all sounds with a collective hush
    not silence but
the quiet grinding of machinary
in which we have no say

beneath the constant energy of hate
each one becomes like
    music in an orchestral brain
that slowly tries to tune
    to an alien sound
the half forgotten interludes
    of complaint
between the shouting and the pain

until the sounds are like the swelling of the sea
the constant background of the spray
    like the grinding of a billion waves
blending into one emphatic note

that pure note of individual souls
    like single waves
that curl back into the collective slumber
    of humanity.

Night chambers

Below mechanical illuminations
    that line the city sky
lie the chambers of the lost
    where the last strays
have found their places
trying to find security
in the collective peace
    that passes

they are the focal point of silence
wrapped in an outer coat of noise
worn out with all the repetition
    of arguments that start
in the secret spaces
    of a mother's thumping heart
that sleepens them to their abandonment

the lost are hidden from those lives above
that make the city their own
    busy and impervious

those closest to them are the most unknown

but in the grace of dreams they hear
strange cries that even the blundering
    of artificial noise cannot cover

these are the sounds
    not of work

    not of the reluctant mechanicals
who keep machines alive
but the moving breathing sleeping discontent
  in which they are all wrapped

like the background gossiping
  of engines overhead
with nothing to say

the sound in its insistent quiet way
drills into the eardrum where it stays
  deeper than distraction
like the quiet background music
  that one cannot quite hear

it is a voice that speaks
in a room of other conversations
  about other lives
more important
  more impervious

it is the hum that seeps out of
the background roar of long distant flight
in the hour that stretches over time
  and bends it
    in the stroking of the curves of earth
beneath the pounding of mechanical intent
the strays are wrapped tightly in the secret spaces
  of their own despair
in their unhappy sleep of the past
hidden from the light
where I join them at last
in the hidden chambers of the night.

Street lights

Even in the blackest night
earth retains the pallor of twilight
    absorbing the last
remnants of the day
    as if it had absconded with the past
and held it to itself

and almost out of sight
the street lamps embedded in their feeble
illuminated patch of comfort
    flicker as if
about to be extinguished
attempting to create
    the small enclosures
safe around a fire
of an almost warmth made visible

as if the comfort of the past
were glimpsed like slits of light
    between the curtains

while the stars spotlight double darkness
    search lights closer home
penetrate the weight of night
seeking out their victims
    in their flight

street lights try again
between the outer darkness and the black below
    to stretch their moments
in the lamplight of time

while in the clouds discomfort rumbles
    above all that seems wrong
a voice sings its suffering
putting all lost childhood into song.

The sounds of achievement

The night is placid
    and the stars
placate the isolation of the earth

 by their their multitude
    and by their distance

between the stars and me
the drone of an unknown aeroplane
heads for somewhere far away
    slowly and very high

its tough reliable engines
    on which all rely
reverberate with sounds that lead
to yearning for those safer places
    far from here

I wonder where the airmen went and why
what destination would await them on the ground
    revelling in their sounds
        like me

who are those lonely souls
isolated in their inner frames of darkness
lulled by the steady sound of engines
purring in mechanical intent
    nearer the stars
and to the welcoming surroundings
    of security
those peaceful places where
all passengers and aircrew land

are the people happier there
were they spared our discontent?

later the bombers and their lonely crews
will expand on their success and safe return
wrapped in their now empty metal frame
their warm bodies in each other's safety
    their journey done
the towns they left behind slowly settling
waiting for the journeys still to come.

Part 2 Lamentations

Foreign Legions

The fields are burdened with their wheat
the mountains heavy with the weight of clouds
    ripe apples palpable as if a painter's hand
       created them

faint sounds of singing drift towards me
    through the heat
       like scattered showers

unregimented voices
    blend in individual tones
join as loosely as a brass band
tuning itself against the elements

I stand still in surprise
    that people will
release their spirits in the air
    without an audience

like unacknowledged birds
scattering their own particulars
    to whom it may concern

and when the sounds of singing near
they become a unison
in rhythms of consolation
    harmonious
       not hierarchical

I hear their song approaching
as naturally as clouds
    that change the landscape every second
with the shadows that belong to wind

the singers are the subjects of the fields
of work required
    not imposed
as natural as hoarded grain
    or the disordered grasses
bent by wind and rain

the workers sing to stay together
using rhythm to share their pain

while the mountains sing of themselves
the sounds of birds
    blend with the almost silent
whisper of the reeds
    and the clouded fields

and in the end the songs
alleviate both rage and fear
    the howls of dying foxes
        and the screams of rutting deer

songs are the voice
of the unleashed heart
    as free as when the birds sing
        not because we want to
            but because we have no choice.

Fishers of men

On the beaches of the past
the fishermen laid nets
like turning fading pages of their time
between the whiff of olive
    and of wine

between the seasons of the moon
and the moody unreliable sea

between the barren sand
and the ancient scrubland of neglect

the sea that was once used by fishermen
is floated in by human flesh as well as fish

and the fishermen have gone
for easier lives
    more latent blame

now they wait
on their fellow men
    netting tips
and all the benefits of shame

the sea has lost its hold
on its old familiar audience
    the sun still folds itself
around new raw and inattentive minds

we wonder what will last
as we become like fearful ancients
      stranded on the beaches of the past.

Bodies

Water clings to its own darkness
    within the harbour walls
all that floats bakes in the sun
and a body drifts face down

men accumulate as subtly as guilt
awkward in the heat
    and with each other
as if outside the church
waiting for the time to submit to it
not wishing to remain excluded
    and unsure of what to do

like unwilling worshippers
who know they should not be there
    they do not wish to miss
the sight that they all share

it is early in the blaze of morning
    and the water still
the body slowly floats towards the quay
back to where it once began

the face is underwater but the clothes
    drying in the sun reveal
the gaudy colours of the night
the pearls or beads
    that lined the contours of delight

the men try not to care
      their eyes lowered
snared in a reluctant fascination
steeped in the harbour's silt
      and half regretted confessions
      as if sharing guilt.

Goose steps

Soldiers in their shiny leather
find their being in each other
feeling justified in all they do
marching as if joined together
knowing their mates will do the same
     a parody of unity

they protect each other against shame
steady as the rhythm of a striking hand
     merciless as anonymity

they bend their heads far back
     as if their eyes
would not see the trodden faces
of what takes place below on earth

pavements echo with the steady beat
of boots beneath the march
     of choreography
treading on anyone below

hatred in an attitude of body
     as well as mind

after the march there is the stillness
     as the soldiers turn to stone
without a flicker of mortality

for all their joint routines
      they are alone
victims of some bidding
      not their own

bullying becomes a state of mind
      the laws of hate
which turn indifference
into someone else's fate.

The burning of the dead

As the curtain closes and the music is
    mechanically nudged
        to be a little louder

mourners shuffle in uncertainty
    judging whether to stay or retire
or return to normal
and the coffin smoothly slides away
in the artificial form of passing on
    accompanied by wood and flowers into the fire

the flames fly with the heat
    forever upwards
        until the soul
disappears in simple purity
unleashed from the soil
    which made it real

after the lingering
    the sparse remembered incidents
distracting listeners
from the other world of their own thoughts

the mourners shuffle off
past the formal handshakes of lamentation
    past the meagre wasted flowers
        wilting in their short extravagance
            fading away too soon

trying not to seem to haste
past the piles of temporary names

the living shake each other's hands

while the timeless words of hope
    still benumb them
with the slightest sense of awe

they are relieved that it is over
uncertainty no different than before.

The moon in daylight

There should be no illusions

stripped of veils of cloud
    the weight of rain
the pitiless blank sky penetrates
all it pounces on
like a fighter's sudden roar nearby
    shattering the stillness
        even when it's gone

but the moon still surprises us
quiet in the outer reaches of the empty air
    beyond the mutability of clouds
sending signals about curves of light
that join the day and night

the moon is like an inner sound
    reflecting rays of someone's fantasy
that leave no trace
for no-one is aware of it
    beyond the realm of distance

we accept the different shades of meaning
      as we acknowledge tides
as if simply there or out of place
but the moon still strikes an awkward note
      as it rises to the upper realms of space
without distinctions that derive from noise
close to the vanished kingdom of heaven
as if it looked down on a younger cousin
      superior as being right

the moon is peopled by imagined symphonies
      each perfect note
heard in purloined harmony

life is cruel

the world has distances
      layers of effects
           the weight of consequences

there is nothing to be trusted

like the moon
the mask of death
      the peace that passes by
into the lost kingdoms of the sky.

Mourning's monument

Unknown soldiers march
to a slow drum beat of the heart
rehearsing their mortality
     in the symbols of impersonality
turning mourning into art

the brass band bleats
the music of oblivion
a symbol of the setting sun
     bells that toll the minor third
that is the sum
of all attempts of consolation

grief is private as
     the loneliness of being human
but mourning is a public duty

soldiers furled in music
    solemn
        dignified
           but not alone

while horses in their own misunderstanding
     wait in animal indifference
for a change of tone

until the anonymous soldiers fire into the air
with perfect timing
    and without intent
like lead toys
    awaiting their own inevitable end

those most honoured in the public eye
retain the status of their birth
high in the layers of humanity
    nearest to heaven
in the hierarchies of the earth
and the reassembly of traditions
where official mourners know their place

while onlookers blend into anonymity
    like a sea
wondering who that special creature was and why
this ceremony is now placed
    in the hierarchies of the sky

perhaps this public figure is leaving
    with relief
the loneliness of being human

is this what God understands as grief?

Paradise on earth

God is everywhere

the micro planets of the soil
    like an internet
communicate through living things
as if the air breathed itself

the tiny plankton
    in the empty richness of unclouded sea
hiding in the idea of colour
    and the flash of lightning
cuts through the stillness of misunderstanding
    reverberating beyond itself

the still small voices of the birds
tolling their songs like bells
the loving contradictions of the lion and the lamb
    teeth and claws
        justice and laws

all this was paradise as it was meant to be

but paradise is overcrowded

all thrived in the world until
the perfect balance between you and me
    became deranged

poised in perfection until
the many were too many and the few too strong

all changed
we had thought contentment was near
even within the reach of prayer

God is everywhere
but here.

Homeland

Home is the place we long for
having left with such sweet confidence
it defines all other places
    by its difference
so why should the heart be so
    uncertain of its whereabouts

why should home be so elusive
    so unfixed
it slips its moorings in the earth
    like friends we never see

what seems as tough as stone
in the shifting footholds of the mind
crumbles into brittle personal bone

the many mansions of a stable heaven
lie beyond the upper reaches of attainment
    like a holy suburb

home gradually becomes unknown
    baroque interiors
spread outwards and forever upwards
    into the empty spaces of eternity

all that was
all this and mine
becomes a passing moment
and reality settles like an aftershock

home is fragile
it changes its perspective
    elusive and never whole

a symbol of displacement
and the universal hunger of the soul.

Displacement

There is a party taking place around me
    as if I were not there
those on either side of me at once
    loud with confidence
flash as lights
    flushed in their own bright
talking at the same time
looking past the other cheeks
    to seek out more important ones
to my cost

I don't belong

and afterwards they tell me
    I was wrong
or did the wrong thing
    like dropping a catch
by which a match was lost

the buzzing in the ears of endless sentences
like the earworm of a song
I am wrong I am wrong I am wrong

I long for where I am supposed to be

that imagined quiet of the lake
    the silence of anticipation
and the soothing of some
    inexplicable
    touch or voice
that creates a there
    there the imagined
study where I used to work

but I am late
and all my papers are displaced

like the flight times and the places
    where I am supposed to be

the promised journeys to the east
forests of larch and pine and ice
    steep banks of rivers
gouged out by the Russian novels
    embrace a form
        I cannot find
the papers that have disappeared
that taught me what I am
    supposed to say

scatter like talk at a cocktail party
where all are sorting out
    the powerpoints of self-display

malfunctioning equipment
gets the better of me and my mind
    and like a guilty thing
I creep away to what I cannot find.

Interior decorations

Early evening is the time
when the secrets of domestic happiness
    present themselves
        inadvertently

before the curtains are drawn
    to keep the darkness out
the insides of small living rooms
    inadvertently
        reveal themselves
in a display for passers by

here are human lives unsealed
reliable as routine
    like watching the TV
or leaving the empty room flickering
to fetch a cup of tea

we see through open curtains
    the isolated light bulb
pictures fading into walls
and the prized anonymous possessions
    safe behind flat glass

from the snug interiors of a car
we glimpse the private satisfaction
of someone else's ordinary bliss
    that like a scene from a film
fades with repetition

or from the slowly moving train we see
    outside the lit interiors
small suburban gardens
    laid to neglect
in a struggle with rubbish
and an underhand exuberance
of weeds
    impersonal
        anonymous
in their possessive overspill

each interior space repeats
    the patinas of black and white
the forced intimacy of artificial light
that does not look like comfort

each room filled with
what will soon be lost
    neglected or ignored

they are the visible landscape of souls
    with their own interior meanings
valuable and sad

what is possessed is rarely cared about
as those things we never had.

Longing

We travel in the realms of hope
    yearning for those places
where apples are ready to be tasted
    and cherries fill the bowls
the liturgies of
lusher meadows on the other side
    of succulence
like tick lists of the mind

where flowing water between rocks forms
    mini kingdoms of repose
upland meadows of wild flowers
    and the undiscovered rose
waiting for the tread of exploration
    in all that is unknown

those who always longed to see
their own places in the sky
take their longing with them
    when they die

those brave enough to long for better things
    like justice or the truth
take their longing to the grave

those who longed to have been loved
    just once
who felt that love would mend them
take their longing to their end

longing lies deeper and more succulent
    than hope
like a glimpse of heaven unattainable
the perfect moment unrepeatable
    that lasts

the people that we never knew
and know it is too late
or knew and left it far too late
    too late
to return into a state of grace

bereft of those lands of orange
and of lemon that we cannot taste
    impatient for security
        without belonging

all that will be left of us
    is longing.

The other world

Exhausted by the day's demands
one desultory afternoon
when all was well
    I found myself
distracted from the pen and paper
    of my mind
watching an old film
    the moving pictures of the past
the black and white
    of ordinary abstract suffering
the public dying
    and the private hell

there in old movies I saw
distracted eyes
    as if they were my own
the trenches and the trench feet
the stubborn suffering of personal defeat

I saw myself there then
dutifully lasting just two weeks
before I fell

an almost cheerful smiling face
        thrown into the flames of time
in a bonfire of humanity

memories from which there is no recovery
        for they are not my own
we cannot choose forgetting
bodies in the mud
simple crosses made of wood

all that was well meant and went so wrong
are histories we do not lose
        and never should.

Casino

Plastic surfaces and gaudy blinds
    the deliberate extinguishing of day
        hour by hour
the tawdry curtains of the mind
    pockmarked with decay
closed off from natural sound and light
    like great minds
        and those with power

pictures of palm trees simulate the shade
    where artificial sun
moves over body shapes
    lying lazy in the haze
        of drinking and the shining lights
blazing the time away

enclosed in such a manufactured world
the dark interiors of souls
cast themselves on the revolving wheel of hope
    the snakes and ladders of despair

croupiers line superior hands with bait
observe the purgatory of ambivalence
with which the individuals cannot cope
    and on which the world depends

this is the malignity of hope

all wait for some external intervention
an announcement of the winner on a show
     when the outcome is already known
        the pause is long
and the many players cower in hope
that their name is on the envelope

    yet

the suspense is prolonged
     into an elongated suffering
        the scope that is given
to manipulate reality and despair

when for a moment of hopeless exploitation
     all could be well

there is no worst

this is the centre of the circles of hell.

Under the sea

The sea is an archaeology of pain
    the cemetery of the unknown
who have no commemoration
    no remains

no rows of chaste white stones
with names and numbers verified
    the pity of waste well organised
        as if such waste were sane

no simple poppies
that multiply like disappearances
    mark out the graves of the sea

below the implacable surface lies another world
where souls went down
    as plentiful
    and as anonymous
as shoals of fish

the seascape of the underworld
    forever strange
where the tears of all the years
harden into sediment

the sea itself is a monument
    to the waste of bodies far below
the souls over whom
the warning bells of war forever toll.